Betty Crocker
Christmas
treats

WILEY

Wiley Publishing, Inc.

General Mills

Publishing Manager: Christine Gray

Editor: Grace Wells

Recipe Development and Testing:
Betty Crocker Kitchens

Photography and Food Styling: General
Mills Photography Studios and Image
Library

Wiley Publishing, Inc.

Publisher: Natalie Chapman

Associate Publisher: Jessica Goodman

Executive Editor: Anne Ficklen

Editor: Meaghan McDonnell

Production Manager: Michael Olivo

Production Editor: Abby Saul

Cover Design: Suzanne Sunwoo

Art Director: Tai Blanche

Layout: Indianapolis Composition
Services

Manufacturing Manager: Kevin Watt

Our Betty Crocker Kitchens seal guar-
antees success in your kitchen. Every
recipe has been tested in America's
Most Trusted Kitchens™ to meet
our high standards of reliability, easy
preparation and great taste.

Find more great ideas at
BettyCrocker.com

Cover photo: Red Velvet Cupcakes
with Marshmallow Buttercream
Frosting (page 78)

Dear Friends

There's no busier time than the Christmas season so let Betty
Crocker help you entertain with ease! Whether you are hosting
a cocktail party, holiday brunch or Christmas dinner, you'll find a
recipe to suit your needs in this collection of festive treats.

Tired of serving the same-old bites and beverages? Recipes like
Festive Cheese Platter and Olive Appetizer Tree will inspire you to
put a holiday twist on classic appetizers. Even beverages can have
a seasonal flair—guests are sure to love "Cran-tinis" and Cinnamon
Cider.

What better way to celebrate with family and friends than a holiday
brunch? Delicious breads like Cranberry Bread and Gingerbread
Muffins will brighten everyone's morning.

And no party is complete without serving something sweet!
Whether you are hosting a cookie exchange or setting up a dessert
buffet, festive cookies are a must at any Christmas gathering.
Round out the dessert buffet with the decadence of a Cherry-
Almond Torte or the decorative fun of a Snowman Cake.

Spread the cheer this holiday season with these great Christmas
Treats!

Warmly,

Betty Crocker

christmas treats

contents

de-stress the holiday season!

The holidays are a season of great anticipation, filled with family, friends and fun. Along with the fun, we tend to have lots of things to do, like shopping, socializing, decorating, baking and cooking. It can seem as though there are more things to do than time to do them. We all tend to recycle our habits, even those causing stress. So, change direction—stepping away from stress creators and stepping toward stress busters is easier than you think. Here are some suggestions:

- Didn't deck the house from stem to stern with holiday decorations? Nobody is checking, and no one will even notice. Instead, concentrate on the areas that give you joy, those that will delight you day and night. Oh, and then there is the food. Ask people to bring something to share, like an appetizer, bread, salad or dessert—or all of these!

- Instead of wrapping all your gifts, use holiday gift bags and colorful tissue paper. The neat thing is that the recipient can reuse the gift bag.

- For the foods you're providing, mix it up between homemade and store-bought or restaurant favorites. Folks care about the effort overall and being together, not whether your rolls or pies were made from scratch.

- Have a cookie exchange with six or eight friends or family members. That way, you need to bake only one kind of cookie, but you'll end up with up six or eight different kinds to store and serve.

So let go a little, relax, enjoy, revel in the day and feel the stress slip away. Above all, remember that the best holiday gifts are your presence and a smile!

cookie baking secrets

- Have at least 3 or 4 cookie sheets on hand so that as you bake one sheet you can get another one ready to go. Use cookie sheets that are at least 2 inches narrower and shorter than the inside dimensions of your oven so heat circulates around them.

- It's best to bake only one cookie sheet at a time, using the middle oven rack. If you want to bake two sheets at the same time, put one on the oven rack in the upper third of the oven and one on the oven rack in the lower third. Remember to switch their positions halfway through the bake time.

- Check cookies at the minimum bake time. Even 1 minute can make a difference with cookies, especially those high in sugar and fat. The longer cookies bake, the more brown, crisp or hard they become.

- Always put cookie dough on completely cooled cookie sheets. Cookies spread too much if put on a hot, or even a warm, cookie sheet. You can cool cookie sheets quickly either by popping them in the refrigerator or freezer or by running cold water over them (dry completely and grease again if needed).

a toast to beverages

Usher in the tidings of the season and be full of good cheer! Holiday entertaining and beverages go hand in hand (turn to Chapter 1 for some great beverage recipes). Whether you're serving wine, cocktails, coffee or hot chocolate, here are some easy ways to jazz them up.

Raise Your Wine Glass

Wine is a year-round favorite. Enjoy it served as is, or "doctor it" a bit.

- Try homemade wine coolers! Mix equal parts of white or light red wine, like rosé, and fruit juice and a shot of fruit-flavored liqueur if you like.

- For mulled wine, add honey and whole spices such as cinnamon, cardamom and cloves to red wine, then heat slowly. Or, look for mulling spices in large specialty kitchen and cookware stores.

Spirited Mixed Drinks

- Make spiked gelatin "poppers." Make any 4-serving-size box of flavored gelatin using 1 cup boiling water. Once gelatin dissolves, stir in ¾ cup rum, brandy, vodka, gin or champagne. Pour into ice-cube trays; refrigerate until set. Remove from the trays to serve.

- Go classic. A traditional dry martini is 1½ to 2 ounces of gin and 2 teaspoons of dry vermouth. Vodka can be substituted for the gin. Shake or stir with ice; strain. Garnish with an olive.

Drink Dazzlers for Mixed Drinks

- Rub rims of glasses with the cut side of a lime or lemon, and then dip into salt or sugar.

- Make ice cubes out of juices for a flavor and color duo.

- Use fresh berries, cherries, citrus twists, kiwifruit slices or melon wedges. Cut a small slit and hook the fruit on the glass rim, or thread fruit on a decorative toothpick and rest it in the glass.

Hot and Cozy Drinks

Tradition, comfort. What better words to describe a mug of hot chocolate or coffee? Explore your options with these ideas:

- For coffee or hot chocolate, stir in about 1 tablespoon chocolate syrup, liqueur, flavored coffee syrup, caramel topping or a scoop of ice cream.

- Add pieces of vanilla bean, a cardamom pod or a cinnamon stick to a pot or cups of coffee or hot chocolate for a spicy flavor and aroma.

Hot and Cozy Drink Dazzlers

- Use a cinnamon stick or peppermint stick as a stirrer.

- Top with whipped cream, and garnish with chocolate-covered coffee beans, grated chocolate, chopped nuts, mini chocolate chips, toasted coconut or crushed candies or cookies. Or drizzle with ice-cream topping.

festive bites and beverages

Baked Coconut Shrimp { About 31 servings }

Prep Time: **40 Minutes**   Start to Finish: **40 Minutes**

¾ cup apricot preserves

2 tablespoons lime juice

½ teaspoon ground mustard

¼ cup all-purpose flour

2 tablespoons packed brown
sugar

¼ teaspoon salt

Dash ground red pepper
(cayenne)

1 egg

1 cup shredded coconut

1 lb uncooked deveined
peeled (with tail shells left
on) medium (31 to 35 count)
shrimp, thawed if frozen

2 tablespoons butter or
margarine, melted

1 In 1-quart saucepan, mix apricot preserves, 1 tablespoon of
the lime juice and the mustard. Cook over low heat, stirring
occasionally, just until preserves are melted. Refrigerate while
making shrimp.

2 Move oven rack to lowest position; heat oven to 425°F. Spray
rack in broiler pan with cooking spray.

3 In shallow bowl, mix flour, brown sugar, salt and red pepper. In
another shallow bowl, beat egg and remaining 1 tablespoon lime
juice. In third shallow bowl, place coconut.

4 Coat each shrimp with flour mixture, then dip each side into
egg mixture and coat well with coconut. Place on rack in broiler
pan. Drizzle with butter.

5 Bake 7 to 8 minutes or until shrimp are pink and coating is
beginning to brown. Serve with preserves mixture.

1 Serving (1 shrimp and 1 teaspoon sauce): Calories 60 (Calories from Fat 20); Total Fat
2g (Saturated Fat 1.5g); Cholesterol 30mg; Sodium 60mg; Total Carbohydrate 8g (Dietary Fiber 0g);
Protein 3g

{
Save yourself from last-minute prep. If you have time,
coat the shrimp up to 2 hours ahead of time. Refrigerate
covered, and bake just before serving.
}

Crab Cakes [6 servings]

Prep Time: **25 Minutes**   Start to Finish: **25 Minutes**

⅓ cup mayonnaise or salad dressing

1 egg

1¼ cups soft bread crumbs (about 2 slices bread)

1 teaspoon ground mustard

¼ teaspoon salt

¼ teaspoon ground red pepper (cayenne), if desired

⅛ teaspoon pepper

2 medium green onions, chopped (2 tablespoons)

3 cans (6 oz each) crabmeat, well drained, cartilage removed and flaked

¼ cup dry bread crumbs

2 tablespoons vegetable oil

1 In medium bowl, mix mayonnaise and egg with whisk. Stir in remaining ingredients except dry bread crumbs and oil. Shape mixture into 6 patties, about 3 inches in diameter (mixture will be moist). Coat each patty with dry bread crumbs.

2 In 12-inch nonstick skillet, heat oil over medium heat. Cook patties in oil about 10 minutes, gently turning once, until golden brown and hot in center. Reduce heat if crab cakes become brown too quickly.

1 Serving: Calories 330 (Calories from Fat 160); Total Fat 18g (Saturated Fat 3g); Cholesterol 120mg; Sodium 690mg; Total Carbohydrate 20g (Dietary Fiber 0g); Protein 22g

Sun-Dried Tomato and Bacon Bruschetta   24 servings

Prep Time: **35 Minutes**   Start to Finish: **50 Minutes**

24 slices (½-inch-thick) baguette French bread (from 10-oz loaf)

½ cup julienne-cut sun-dried tomatoes packed in oil

½ cup chopped cooked bacon

¾ cup finely shredded fontina cheese (2 oz)

¼ cup finely chopped fresh parsley

1 Heat oven to 400°F. In ungreased 15 × 10 × 1-inch pan, place bread slices.

2 In strainer over small bowl, place tomatoes; press tomatoes to drain oil into bowl (2 to 3 tablespoons oil is needed). Brush oil on bread. Bake 5 to 7 minutes or until crisp.

3 Top bread slices with tomatoes, bacon and cheese. Bake about 5 minutes or until cheese is melted. Sprinkle with parsley. Serve warm.

1 Serving: Calories 70 (Calories from Fat 20); Total Fat 2.5g (Saturated Fat 1g); Cholesterol 0mg; Sodium 150mg; Total Carbohydrate 9g (Dietary Fiber 0g); Protein 3g

Fruit Bruschetta [28 bruschetta]

Prep Time: **15 Minutes**   Start to Finish: **15 Minutes**

1 package (10.75 oz) frozen pound cake loaf, cut into fourteen ½-inch slices

⅔ cup strawberry, raspberry or pineapple cream cheese spread (from 8-oz container)

1 can (11 oz) mandarin orange segments, well drained

56 bite-size pieces assorted fresh fruit (kiwifruit, strawberry, raspberry, pear, apple)

Chocolate-flavor syrup, if desired

Toasted coconut or sliced almonds, if desired

1 Set oven control to broil. Place cake slices on rack in broiler pan. Broil with tops 4 to 5 inches from heat 3 to 5 minutes, turning once, until light golden brown.

2 Spread each cake slice with about 2 teaspoons cream cheese spread. Cut slices diagonally in half to make 28 pieces. Top with orange segments and desired fruit. Drizzle with syrup; sprinkle with coconut.

1 Bruschetta: Calories 90 (Calories from Fat 45); Total Fat 5g (Saturated Fat 2.5g); Cholesterol 15mg; Sodium 30mg; Total Carbohydrate 11g (Dietary Fiber 1g); Protein 1g

Winter Fruit Kabobs with Peach Glaze   16 kabobs

Prep Time: **35 Minutes**   Start to Finish: **35 Minutes**

16 skewers (8 inch)

6 cups bite-size pieces assorted fresh fruit (pineapple, pears, apples, kiwifruit, strawberries)

2 cups grapes

¾ cup peach or apricot preserves

2 tablespoons butter or margarine

2 tablespoons orange-flavored liqueur or orange juice

¼ teaspoon ground cinnamon

1   On each skewer, thread 4 to 6 pieces of fruit, including grapes. Place skewers on large cookie sheet; set aside.

2   In 1-quart saucepan, heat preserves, butter, liqueur and cinnamon over medium-high heat, stirring frequently, until butter is melted. Brush about ¼ to ⅓ cup of preserves mixture over kabobs; reserve remaining preserves mixture.

3   Set oven control to broil. Broil kabobs with tops 4 to 6 inches from heat 2 minutes or until fruit is hot and glaze is bubbly. Serve warm or cold with remaining preserves mixture.

1 Kabob: Calories 110 (Calories from Fat 15); Total Fat 2g (Saturated Fat 1g); Cholesterol 0mg; Sodium 15mg; Total Carbohydrate 22g (Dietary Fiber 2g); Protein 0g

If you're using bamboo skewers, soak them in water at least 30 minutes before using to prevent burning.

Antipasto Platter   24 servings

Prep Time: **30 Minutes**   Start to Finish: **30 Minutes**

12 slices prosciutto or thinly
sliced fully cooked ham
(about 6 oz), cut in half

12 slices provolone cheese
(about ¾ lb), cut in half

24 thin slices Genoa salami
(about ¾ lb)

24 marinated mushrooms

24 marinated artichoke hearts

24 kalamata olives, pitted

⅓ cup olive or vegetable oil

¼ cup lemon juice

1 tablespoon chopped fresh or
½ teaspoon dried oregano
leaves

12 slices hard-crusted round
Italian bread or 24 slices
French bread (½ inch thick)

1 On large platter, arrange all ingredients except oil, lemon juice, oregano and bread.

2 In small bowl, mix oil, lemon juice and oregano. Drizzle over meats, cheese and vegetables.

3 If using Italian bread, cut each slice in half. On large plate, arrange bread. Serve with meats, cheese and vegetables.

1 Serving: Calories 180 (Calories from Fat 120); Total Fat 13g (Saturated Fat 5g); Cholesterol 25mg; Sodium 610mg; Total Carbohydrate 7g (Dietary Fiber 0g); Protein 10g

Cut the bread into cubes and thread with the other
ingredients onto skewers. Stand the skewers up in a pitcher
or clean vase to add height and drama to a buffet.

Festive Cheese Platter 16 servings

Prep Time: **25 Minutes**   Start to Finish: **25 Minutes**

16 slices (1 oz each) assorted
   cheeses (such as Cheddar,
   Colby–Monterey Jack,
   pepper Jack and Swiss)

½ cup salted roasted whole
   almonds

16 crackers

1 Cut cheese with 2-inch tree, Santa, snowman, star or other cookie cutter in holiday shape. Leftover pieces of cheese can be used in other recipes like nachos, macaroni and cheese or omelets.

2 On medium platter, arrange cheese, overlapping shapes slightly. Sprinkle with almonds. Serve with crackers.

1 Serving: Calories 160 (Calories from Fat 120); Total Fat 13g (Saturated Fat 6g); Cholesterol 30mg; Sodium 220mg; Total Carbohydrate 3g (Dietary Fiber 0g); Protein 8g

Festive Fruit and Cheese Platter Omit purchased sliced cheese. Cut two 8-oz blocks assorted cheeses (such as Cheddar, Colby–Monterey Jack or Swiss) crosswise into ¼-inch-thick slices; place on platter. Arrange 1 pint (2 cups) small whole strawberries, 1 cup each whole green and red grapes, 1 medium unpeeled apple, sliced, and 1 medium unpeeled pear, sliced, on platter with cheese. Brush apple and pear slices with lemon or orange juice to prevent them from turning brown. Makes 18 to 20 servings.

Tex-Mex Cheese Platter Omit purchased sliced cheese. Cut two 8-oz blocks assorted cheeses (such as Cheddar, Colby–Monterey Jack or Pepper Jack) into 1-inch cubes; place on platter. Arrange 1 cup each whole ripe olives and pimiento-stuffed olives on platter with cheese. Drizzle lightly with salsa, and garnish with fresh cilantro leaves. Makes 18 to 20 servings.

Top to bottom: Festive Fruit and Cheese Platter, Tex-Mex Cheese Platter and Festive Cheese Platter.

Olive Appetizer Tree   30 servings

Prep Time: **55 Minutes**   Start to Finish: **55 Minutes**

1 bottle (10 oz) small
  pimiento-stuffed olives

1 bottle (10 oz) large
  pimiento-stuffed olives

6 oz pitted kalamata or ripe
  olives

1 block (1 lb) Colby cheese

1 package (125-count)
  toothpicks

1 cone shape (9 inches tall)
  green or white floral foam

1   Drain olives. Cut block of cheese horizontally into 2 pieces, each
        about ½ inch thick. Cut cheese with 1-inch star-shape canapé or
        cookie cutter. Cover cheese stars with plastic wrap.

2   Break toothpicks in half as needed. Starting at bottom of cone,
        insert toothpicks in random order until they stay securely in
        place. Push each olive onto toothpick half. When placing olives
        around the tree, vary the olive sizes and leave spaces for the
        cheese stars. For stability of the tree, place most of the larger
        olives near the bottom.

3   Push each cheese star onto toothpick half; insert into cone
        among the olives. Top tree with a cheese star that has been
        inserted horizontally on toothpick between points of star.
        Serve immediately or cover loosely and refrigerate no longer
        than 8 hours before serving.

1 Serving (3 pieces): Calories 80 (Calories from Fat 60); Total Fat 7g (Saturated Fat 3g);
Cholesterol 15mg; Sodium 350mg; Total Carbohydrate 1g (Dietary Fiber 0g); Protein 3g

CLICK!

For more festive appetizer recipes, go to
www.bettycrocker.com/appetizers.

"Cran-tinis" { 4 servings }

Prep Time: **5 Minutes**   Start to Finish: **5 Minutes**

1 cup cranberry juice (8 oz)

½ cup citrus vodka or plain vodka (4 oz)

¼ cup Triple Sec or orange juice (2 oz)

1 teaspoon fresh lime juice

1 Fill martini shaker or 3-cup covered container half full with ice. Add all ingredients except cranberries and lime slices; cover and shake.

2 Pour into martini or tall stemmed glasses, straining the ice.

1 Serving (about ½ cup each): Calories 45 (Calories from Fat 0); Total Fat 0g (Saturated Fat 0g); Cholesterol 0mg; Sodium 0mg; Total Carbohydrate 11g (Dietary Fiber 0g); Protein 0g

Pretty in pink describes the beautiful blushing hue of this very hip version of the classic martini. Cran-tinis are sweeter than regular martinis, so true martini drinkers may want to cut the cranberry juice in half. For a slightly less potent drink, serve Cran-tinis on the rocks and add a splash of sparkling water.

Garnish each drink by skewering fresh cranberries on a toothpick and placing the skewer and a strip of lime peel in the bottom of each glass.

Quick Cranberry Punch

24 servings

Prep Time: **5 Minutes**   Start to Finish: **5 Minutes**

1 can (12 oz) frozen lemonade concentrate, thawed

1½ cups cold water

1 bottle (64 oz) cranberry juice cocktail, chilled

4 cans (12 oz each) ginger ale, chilled

Ice ring (see below) or ice

1 In pitcher, mix lemonade concentrate and water.

2 Just before serving, pour lemonade into large punch bowl. Stir in cranberry juice cocktail and ginger ale. Add ice ring.

1 Serving (¾ cup): Calories 100 (Calories from Fat 0); Total Fat 0g (Saturated Fat 0g); Cholesterol 0mg; Sodium 10mg; Total Carbohydrate 24g (Dietary Fiber 0g); Protein 0g

Ice Ring Make a frosty ice ring by filling a ring mold or fluted tube cake pan with crushed ice (the mold needs to be smaller than your punch bowl). Cut fruit such as lemons, limes, oranges and starfruit into ½-inch slices; arrange in the ice so the fruit sticks up above the top of the mold. Or cut citrus peel into star shapes, using tiny cookie cutters. Freeze the mold 15 minutes, then slowly add cold water, some of the punch or fruit juice to fill the mold. Freeze overnight or until solid. When you're ready to serve the punch, run hot water over the bottom of the mold to loosen the ice ring. Remove the ice ring and float it in the punch. Or with the same technique, use muffin cups to make floating ice disks, which take less time to freeze.

Make ice cubes with some of your punch recipe or use just juice instead of water. When the juice cubes melt, the punch won't be diluted.

Holiday Eggnog   6 servings

Prep Time: **30 Minutes**   Start to Finish: **30 Minutes**

3 eggs, slightly beaten	½ cup rum, if desired
⅓ cup granulated sugar	1 cup heavy whipping cream
Dash salt	1 tablespoon packed brown sugar
2½ cups milk	Ground nutmeg
1 teaspoon vanilla	

1 In heavy 2-quart saucepan, mix eggs, granulated sugar and salt. Gradually stir in milk. Cook over low heat 15 to 20 minutes, stirring constantly, just until mixture coats a metal spoon; remove from heat. Stir in vanilla and rum. Keep warm.

2 Just before serving, in chilled small bowl, beat whipping cream and brown sugar with electric mixer on high speed until stiff. Gently stir 1 cup of the whipped cream into eggnog mixture.

3 Pour eggnog into small heatproof punch bowl. Drop remaining whipped cream into 4 or 5 mounds onto eggnog. Sprinkle nutmeg on whipped cream mounds. Serve immediately. Cover and refrigerate any remaining eggnog.

1 Serving (about ¾ cup): Calories 260 (Calories from Fat 150); Total Fat 17g (Saturated Fat 10g); Cholesterol 160mg; Sodium 135mg; Total Carbohydrate 20g (Dietary Fiber 0g); Protein 7g

Hot Cappuccino Eggnog Substitute coffee liqueur for the rum, and add 1 cup hot espresso coffee.

Love the flavor of eggnog but not the calories? Substitute 2 eggs plus 2 egg whites for the 3 eggs, and 2¼ cups fat-free (skim) milk for the milk. Instead of the beaten whipping cream and brown sugar, use 2 cups frozen (thawed) fat-free whipped topping.

CLICK!

For more great drink recipes, go to www .bettycrocker.com/drinks.

Cinnamon Cider

32 servings

Prep Time: **35 Minutes**   Start to Finish: **35 Minutes**

1 gallon apple cider
⅔ cup sugar
2 teaspoons whole allspice
2 teaspoons whole cloves

2 cinnamon sticks, 3 inches long
2 oranges, studded with cloves

1   In 4-quart Dutch oven, heat all ingredients except oranges to boiling; reduce heat. Cover; simmer 20 minutes.

2   Strain punch through sieve or colander. Pour into small heatproof punch bowl. Float oranges in bowl. Serve hot.

1 Serving (½ cup): Calories 80 (Calories from Fat 0); Total Fat 0g (Saturated Fat 0g); Cholesterol 0mg; Sodium 0mg; Total Carbohydrate 19g (Dietary Fiber 0g); Protein 0g

Cinnamon Cider Floats Make cider as directed—except omit oranges with cloves. Place a scoop of cinnamon or vanilla ice cream in each of 32 large serving mugs; add hot cider and garnish with additional cinnamon sticks if desired.

> Pull out the slow cooker to help you with the holidays. When serving hot cider at a holiday buffet, pour heated cider into a slow cooker set on Low, and let guests help themselves. If you prefer to keep the hot cider in the kitchen, keep the cider in an attractive saucepan right on the stove over low heat. Invite guests into the kitchen to ladle it into their own mugs.

holiday breads

Chai-Spiced Bread

1 loaf (16 slices)

Prep Time: **15 Minutes**   Start to Finish: **3 Hours 55 Minutes**

BREAD

¾ cup granulated sugar

½ cup butter or margarine, softened

½ cup prepared tea or water

⅓ cup milk

2 teaspoons vanilla

2 eggs

2 cups all-purpose flour

2 teaspoons baking powder

¾ teaspoon ground cardamom

½ teaspoon salt

¼ teaspoon ground cinnamon

⅛ teaspoon ground cloves

GLAZE

1 cup powdered sugar

¼ teaspoon vanilla

3 to 5 teaspoons milk

Additional ground cinnamon

1 Heat oven to 400°F. Grease bottom only of 8 × 4- or 9 × 5-inch loaf pan with shortening or cooking spray.

2 In large bowl, beat granulated sugar and butter with electric mixer on medium speed until fluffy. On low speed, beat in tea, ⅓ cup milk, 2 teaspoons vanilla and the eggs until ingredients are well combined (mixture will appear curdled). Stir in remaining bread ingredients just until moistened. Spread in pan.

3 Bake 50 to 60 minutes or until toothpick inserted in center comes out clean (do not underbake). Cool in pan on cooling rack 10 minutes. Loosen sides of loaf from pan; remove from pan to cooling rack. Cool 30 minutes.

4 In small bowl, stir powdered sugar, ¼ teaspoon vanilla and 3 teaspoons of the milk, adding more milk by teaspoonfuls, until spreadable. Spread glaze over bread. Sprinkle with additional cinnamon. Cool completely, about 2 hours, before slicing. Wrap tightly and store at room temperature up to 4 days, or refrigerate up to 10 days.

1 Slice: Calories 190 (Calories from Fat 60); Total Fat 7g (Saturated Fat 4g); Cholesterol 40mg; Sodium 190mg; Total Carbohydrate 30g (Dietary Fiber 0g); Protein 3g

Cranberry Bread 2 loaves (24 slices each)

Prep Time: **15 Minutes**   Start to Finish: **3 Hours 30 Minutes**

3 cups fresh or frozen
(thawed) cranberries

1⅔ cups granulated sugar

⅔ cup vegetable oil

½ cup milk

2 teaspoons grated orange or
lemon peel

2 teaspoons vanilla

4 eggs

3 cups all-purpose or whole
wheat flour

2 teaspoons baking soda

1 teaspoon salt

½ teaspoon baking powder

½ cup coarsely chopped nuts

1 Heat the oven to 350°F. Spray just the bottoms of two
8 × 4-inch loaf pans with the cooking spray.

2 In large bowl, stir cranberries, sugar, oil, milk, orange peel,
vanilla and eggs with wooden spoon until well mixed. Stir in
remaining ingredients. Divide batter evenly between pans.

3 Bake 1 hour to 1 hour 5 minutes or until toothpick inserted
in center comes out clean. Cool 10 minutes in pans on
cooling rack.

4 Run small knife or metal spatula along sides of breads to loosen
loaves. Remove from pans to cooling rack. Cool completely,
about 2 hours, before slicing. Wrap tightly; store at room
temperature up to 4 days, or refrigerate up to 10 days.

1 Slice: Calories 100 (Calories from Fat 40); Total Fat 4.5g (Saturated Fat 0.5g); Cholesterol 20mg;
Sodium 115mg; Total Carbohydrate 14g (Dietary Fiber 0g); Protein 2g

Pumpkin Bread { 2 loaves (24 slices each) }

Prep Time: **15 Minutes**   Start to Finish: **3 Hours 25 Minutes**

1 can (15 oz) pumpkin (not pumpkin pie mix)

1⅔ cups sugar

⅔ cup vegetable oil

2 teaspoons vanilla

4 eggs

3 cups all-purpose or whole wheat flour

2 teaspoons baking soda

1 teaspoon salt

1 teaspoon ground cinnamon

½ teaspoon ground cloves

½ teaspoon baking powder

½ cup coarsely chopped nuts

½ cup raisins, if desired

1 Move oven rack to low position so that tops of pans will be in center of oven. Heat oven to 350°F. Grease bottoms only of two 8 × 4-inch loaf pans or one 9 × 5-inch loaf pan with shortening or cooking spray.

2 In large bowl, stir pumpkin, sugar, oil, vanilla and eggs until well mixed. Stir in remaining ingredients except nuts and raisins. Stir in nuts and raisins. Divide batter evenly between 8-inch pans or pour into 9-inch pan.

3 Bake 8-inch loaves 50 to 60 minutes, 9-inch loaf 1 hour 10 minutes to 1 hour 20 minutes, or until toothpick inserted in center comes out clean. Cool 10 minutes in pans on cooling rack.

4 Loosen sides of loaves from pans; remove from pans to cooling rack. Cool completely, about 2 hours, before slicing. Wrap tightly and store at room temperature up to 4 days, or refrigerate up to 10 days.

1 Slice: Calories 100 (Calories from Fat 40); Total Fat 4.5g (Saturated Fat 0.5g); Cholesterol 20mg; Sodium 115mg; Total Carbohydrate 14g (Dietary Fiber 0g); Protein 2g

Zucchini Bread Substitute 3 cups shredded unpeeled zucchini (2 to 3 medium) for the pumpkin.

Chocolate-Pistachio Bread

1 loaf (24 slices)

Prep Time: **15 Minutes**   Start to Finish: **4 Hours 35 Minutes**

⅔ cup granulated sugar	½ cup semisweet chocolate chips
½ cup butter or margarine, melted	⅓ cup unsweetened baking cocoa
¾ cup milk	2 teaspoons baking powder
1 egg	¼ teaspoon salt
1½ cups all-purpose flour	Decorator sugar crystals, if desired
1 cup chopped pistachio nuts	

1 Heat oven to 350°F. Generously grease bottom of 9 × 5-inch glass or shiny metal loaf pan with shortening; do not use dark-colored bakeware or bread will burn around edges. In large bowl, mix granulated sugar, butter, milk and egg until well blended. Stir in remaining ingredients except sugar crystals. Pour into pan. Sprinkle with sugar crystals.

2 Bake 60 to 70 minutes or until toothpick inserted in center comes out clean. Cool 10 minutes in pan on cooling rack.

3 Loosen sides of loaf from pan; remove from pan to cooling rack. Cool completely, about 3 hours, before slicing.

1 Slice: Calories 150 (Calories from Fat 70); Total Fat 8g (Saturated Fat 3g); Cholesterol 20mg; Sodium 120mg; Total Carbohydrate 16g (Dietary Fiber 1g); Protein 3g

Double Chocolate–Walnut Bread Substitute chocolate milk for regular milk and walnuts for the pistachio nuts.

To make ahead, bake and cool the loaf, wrap it tightly and refrigerate up to 10 days or freeze up to 3 months.

Pull-Apart Caramel Loaf   6 servings

Prep Time: **10 Minutes**   Start to Finish: **2 Hours 50 Minutes**

6 frozen cinnamon rolls (from 36.5-oz bag)

½ cup packed brown sugar

¼ cup butter or margarine

2 tablespoons light corn syrup

2 tablespoons whipping cream

1   Heat oven to 175°F. Place rolls on cutting board. Let stand 10 minutes or until partially thawed.

2   Meanwhile, in 1-quart saucepan, heat brown sugar and butter over medium heat, stirring constantly, until butter is melted. Stir in corn syrup and whipping cream. Pour brown sugar mixture into 9 × 5-inch loaf pan, covering bottom completely.

3   Cut each cinnamon roll in half crosswise. Arrange roll halves randomly over brown sugar mixture in pan. Cover loosely with plastic wrap sprayed with cooking spray. Place pan in oven and turn off heat. Let rise 1 hour 10 minutes to 1 hour 30 minutes or until loaf has at least doubled in size and top of loaf is 1 inch from top of pan. Remove from oven.

4   Heat oven to 350°F. Remove plastic wrap. Bake loaf 25 to 30 minutes or until golden brown. Place heatproof tray or serving plate upside down over pan; immediately turn tray and pan over. Let pan remain 1 minute so caramel can drizzle over loaf; remove pan. Serve warm.

1 Serving: Calories 380 (Calories from Fat 150); Total Fat 17g (Saturated Fat 8g); Cholesterol 40mg; Sodium 210mg; Total Carbohydrate 53g (Dietary Fiber 1g); Protein 4g

If you like pecans, add chopped pecans to the caramel mixture in the pan.

Fresh Raspberry Coffee Cake

9 servings

Prep Time: **20 Minutes**   Start to Finish: **1 Hour 10 Minutes**

COFFEE CAKE

½ cup butter or margarine, melted

¾ cup milk

1 teaspoon vanilla

1 egg

2 cups all-purpose flour

½ cup granulated sugar

2 teaspoons baking powder

½ teaspoon salt

1 cup fresh raspberries

GLAZE

½ cup powdered sugar

1 tablespoon butter or margarine, softened

2 to 3 teaspoons water

¼ teaspoon almond extract

1 Heat oven to 400°F. Spray 9- or 8-inch square pan with baking spray with flour.

2 In medium bowl, beat ½ cup butter, the milk, vanilla and egg with spoon. Stir in flour, granulated sugar, baking powder and salt just until flour is moistened. Fold in raspberries. Spread in pan.

3 Bake 25 to 30 minutes or until top is golden brown and toothpick inserted in center comes out clean. Cool 20 minutes.

4 In small bowl, mix glaze ingredients until smooth and thin enough to drizzle. Drizzle glaze over warm coffee cake.

1 Serving: Calories 300 (Calories from Fat 120); Total Fat 13g (Saturated Fat 8g); Cholesterol 55mg; Sodium 340mg; Total Carbohydrate 42g (Dietary Fiber 1g); Protein 5g

This coffee cake is best served warm, but you can microwave a piece for 10 to 15 seconds on High to bring back that fresh-from-the-oven taste.

Sour Cream Coffee Cake

Prep Time: **30 Minutes**   Start to Finish: **2 Hours**

BROWN SUGAR FILLING

½ cup packed brown sugar

½ cup finely chopped nuts

1½ teaspoons ground cinnamon

COFFEE CAKE

3 cups all-purpose or whole wheat flour

1½ teaspoons baking powder

1½ teaspoons baking soda

¾ teaspoon salt

1½ cups granulated sugar

¾ cup butter or margarine, softened

1½ teaspoons vanilla

3 eggs

1½ cups sour cream

GLAZE

½ cup powdered sugar

¼ teaspoon vanilla

2 to 3 teaspoons milk

1 Heat oven to 350°F. Grease bottom and side of 10 × 4-inch angel food (tube) cake pan, 12-cup fluted tube cake pan or two 9 × 5-inch loaf pans with shortening or cooking spray.

2 In small bowl, stir all filling ingredients until well mixed; set aside. In large bowl, stir flour, baking powder, baking soda and salt until well mixed; set aside.

3 In another large bowl, beat granulated sugar, butter, 1½ teaspoons vanilla and eggs with electric mixer on medium speed 2 minutes, scraping bowl occasionally. Beat about one-fourth of the flour mixture and sour cream at a time alternately into sugar mixture on low speed until blended.

4 For angel food or fluted tube cake pan, spread one-third of the batter (about 2 cups) in pan, then sprinkle with one-third of the filling; repeat twice. For loaf pans, spread one-fourth of the batter (about 1½ cups) in each pan, then sprinkle each with one-fourth of the filling; repeat once.

5 Bake angel food or fluted tube cake pan about 1 hour, loaf pans about 45 minutes, or until toothpick inserted near center comes out clean. Cool 10 minutes in pan(s) on cooling rack. Remove from pan(s) to cooling rack. Cool 20 minutes. In small bowl, stir all glaze ingredients until smooth and thin enough to drizzle. Drizzle glaze over coffee cake. Serve warm or cool.

1 Serving: Calories 360 (Calories from Fat 150); Total Fat 16g (Saturated Fat 8g); Cholesterol 75mg; Sodium 360mg; Total Carbohydrate 49g (Dietary Fiber 1g); Protein 5g

{ The classics never go out of style, so you just can't go wrong with this superb-tasting, moist coffee cake. }

Almond–Poppy Seed Muffins

12 muffins

Prep Time: **15 Minutes**   Start to Finish: **35 Minutes**

MUFFINS
½ cup sugar
⅓ cup vegetable oil
1 egg
½ teaspoon almond extract
½ cup sour cream
¼ cup milk
1⅓ cups all-purpose flour

½ teaspoon baking powder
½ teaspoon salt
¼ teaspoon baking soda
2 tablespoons poppy seed

TOPPING
3 teaspoons sugar
2 tablespoons sliced almonds

1 Heat the oven to 375°F. Place a paper baking cup in each of 12 regular-size muffin cups, or spray with cooking spray.

2 In large bowl, stir together ½ cup sugar, the oil, egg and almond extract. Beat in sour cream and milk with spoon until blended. Stir in flour, baking powder, salt, baking soda and poppy seed just until blended. Divide batter evenly among muffin cups. Sprinkle batter with 3 teaspoons sugar and the almonds.

3 Bake 14 to 17 minutes or until toothpick inserted in center comes out clean. If muffins were baked in paper baking cups immediately remove from pan to cooling rack. If muffins were baked in sprayed pan, leave in pan about 5 minutes, then remove from pan to cooling rack. Serve warm or cooled.

1 Muffin: Calories 180 (Calories from Fat 90); Total Fat 10g (Saturated Fat 2.5g); Cholesterol 25mg; Sodium 160mg; Total Carbohydrate 21g (Dietary Fiber 0g); Protein 3g

Gingerbread Muffins

12 muffins

Prep Time: **15 Minutes** Start to Finish: **35 Minutes**

¼ cup packed brown sugar	1 teaspoon baking powder
½ cup molasses	1 teaspoon ground ginger
⅓ cup milk	½ teaspoon salt
⅓ cup vegetable oil	½ teaspoon baking soda
1 egg	½ teaspoon ground cinnamon
2 cups all-purpose flour	¼ teaspoon ground allspice

1 Heat oven to 400°F. Grease bottoms only of 12 regular-size muffin cups with shortening, or place paper baking cup in each muffin cup.

2 In large bowl, beat brown sugar, molasses, milk, oil and egg with spoon. Stir in remaining ingredients just until flour is moistened. Divide batter evenly among muffin cups.

3 Bake 18 to 20 minutes or until toothpick inserted in center comes out clean. Immediately remove from pan to cooling rack. Serve warm if desired.

1 Muffin: Calories 200 (Calories from Fat 60); Total Fat 7g (Saturated Fat 1g); Cholesterol 20mg; Sodium 210mg; Total Carbohydrate 32g (Dietary Fiber 0g); Protein 3g

For a festive holiday finish, try these ideas:

- Dip muffin tops into melted butter and then into a mixture of ground cinnamon and sugar.
- Drizzle tops with melted white vanilla baking chips.
- Slice muffins in half, and fill with vanilla pudding or ice cream. Top with caramel or lemon sauce, and sprinkle with ground cinnamon or nutmeg.

For an easy-on-the-budget Jolly Holiday Brunch menu including party guide and recipes, go to www.bettycrocker .com/holidaybrunch

Scones { 8 scones }

Prep Time: **15 Minutes**   Start to Finish: **35 Minutes**

1¾ cups all-purpose flour

3 tablespoons granulated sugar

2½ teaspoons baking powder

½ teaspoon salt

⅓ cup cold butter or margarine

1 egg

½ teaspoon vanilla

4 to 6 tablespoons whipping cream

Additional 1 tablespoon whipping cream

2 teaspoons white decorator sugar crystals or granulated sugar

1 Heat oven to 400°F. In large bowl, stir flour, 3 tablespoons sugar, the baking powder and salt until mixed. Cut in butter, using pastry blender or fork, until mixture looks like fine crumbs. Stir in egg, vanilla and just enough of the 4 to 6 tablespoons whipping cream until mixture forms a soft dough and leaves the side of the bowl.

2 Place dough on lightly floured surface; gently roll in flour to coat. Knead 10 times. On ungreased cookie sheet, roll or pat dough into 8-inch round. Cut into 8 wedges with sharp knife dipped in sugar but do not separate wedges. Brush with additional whipping cream; sprinkle with sugar crystals.

3 Bake 14 to 16 minutes or until light golden brown. Immediately remove from cookie sheet to cooling rack; carefully separate wedges. Serve warm.

1 Scone: Calories 230 (Calories from Fat 100); Total Fat 11g (Saturated Fat 7g); Cholesterol 55mg; Sodium 370mg; Total Carbohydrate 27g (Dietary Fiber 0g); Protein 4g

Chocolate Chip Scones Stir in ½ cup miniature semisweet chocolate chips with the egg, vanilla and whipping cream in step 2.

Currant Scones Stir in ½ cup currants or raisins with the egg, vanilla and whipping cream in step 2.

Easy Drop Danish 12 Danish

Prep Time: **15 Minutes** . Start to Finish: **30 Minutes**

DANISH	VANILLA GLAZE
2 cups Original Bisquick® mix	¾ cup powdered sugar
¼ cup butter or margarine, softened	1 tablespoon warm water
2 tablespoons granulated sugar	¼ teaspoon vanilla
⅔ cup milk	
¼ cup apricot preserves (or other flavor fruit preserves)	

1 Heat oven to 450°F. Lightly grease cookie sheet with shortening or cooking spray. In medium bowl, stir Bisquick mix, butter and sugar until crumbly. Stir in milk until dough forms; beat 15 strokes.

2 Drop dough by rounded tablespoonfuls about 2 inches apart onto cookie sheet. Make a shallow well in center of each with back of spoon; fill each with 1 teaspoon preserves.

3 Bake 10 to 15 minutes or until golden brown.

4 In small bowl, mix all glaze ingredients with spoon until smooth and thin enough to drizzle. Drizzle glaze over warm Danish.

1 Danish: Calories 180 (Calories from Fat 60); Total Fat 7g (Saturated Fat 3g); Cholesterol 10mg; Sodium 320mg; Total Carbohydrate 27g (Dietary Fiber 0g); Protein 2g

Easy Cherry-Almond Danish Substitute cherry preserves for the apricot preserves and almond extract for the vanilla in the vanilla glaze. For a nutty crunch, sprinkle the glaze with toasted chopped almonds.

Tuck this recipe in your "never-fails" folder. These Danish look so pretty and fancy yet are very simple to throw together. Alternate the filling with various types of jam and jelly— they'll look especially lovely on a serving tray this way.

3

festive cookies

Season's Best Sugar Cookies

{ About 5 dozen cookies }

Prep Time: **1 Hour**   Start to Finish: **3 Hours**

COOKIES

1½ cups powdered sugar

1 cup butter or margarine, softened

1 teaspoon vanilla

½ teaspoon almond extract

1 egg

2½ cups all-purpose flour

1 teaspoon baking soda

1 teaspoon cream of tartar

WHITE GLAZE

2 cups powdered sugar

2 tablespoons milk

¼ teaspoon almond extract

Sprinkles

Red edible glitter or red sugar

1 In large bowl, beat 1½ cups powdered sugar and the butter with electric mixer on medium speed, or mix with spoon. Stir in vanilla, ½ teaspoon almond extract and the egg. Stir in flour, baking soda and cream of tartar. Cover and refrigerate about 2 hours or until firm.

2 Heat oven to 375°F. On lightly floured cloth-covered surface, roll half of dough at a time ⅛ inch thick. Cut into candy cane or other desired shapes. On ungreased cookie sheets, place 2 inches apart.

3 Bake 7 to 8 minutes or until light brown. Remove from cookie sheet to cooling rack. Cool completely.

4 Mix glaze ingredients until smooth and desired spreading consistency, adding a few extra drops milk if needed. Spread glaze over cookies. Sprinkle with glitter or sugars.

1 Cookie: Calories 80 (Calories from Fat 30); Total Fat 3g (Saturated Fat 2g); Cholesterol 10mg; Sodium 45mg; Total Carbohydrate 11g (Dietary Fiber 0g); Protein 0g

CLICK!

For a Christmas Cookie Exchange menu including party guide and recipes, go to www.bettycrocker.com/cookieexchange

Raspberry Poinsettia Blossoms

3 dozen cookies

Prep Time: **25 Minutes**   Start to Finish: **1 Hour 50 Minutes**

¾ cup butter or margarine, softened

½ cup sugar

1 teaspoon vanilla

1 box (4-serving size) raspberry-flavored gelatin

1 egg

2 cups all-purpose flour

2 tablespoons yellow candy sprinkles

1 In large bowl, beat butter, sugar, vanilla, gelatin and egg with electric mixer on medium speed, or mix with spoon. On low speed, beat in flour.

2 Shape dough into 1¼-inch balls. Cover and refrigerate 1 hour.

3 Heat oven to 375°F. On ungreased cookie sheets, place balls about 2 inches apart. With sharp knife, make 6 cuts in top of each ball about three-fourths of the way through to make 6 wedges. Spread wedges apart slightly to form flower petals (cookies will separate and flatten as they bake). Sprinkle about ⅛ teaspoon yellow candy sprinkles into center of each cookie.

4 Bake 9 to 11 minutes or until set and edges begin to brown. Cool 2 to 3 minutes. Remove from cookie sheets to cooling rack. Cool completely, about 15 minutes.

1 Cookie: Calories 90 (Calories from Fat 40); Total Fat 4g (Saturated Fat 2.5g); Cholesterol 15mg; Sodium 40mg; Total Carbohydrate 11g (Dietary Fiber 0g); Protein 1g

For a flavor twist, use strawberry-, cranberry- or cherry-flavored gelatin instead of the raspberry.

Espresso Thumbprint Cookies

{ About 3½ dozen cookies }

Prep Time: **1 Hour 30 Minutes**   Start to Finish: **1 Hour 45 Minutes**

COOKIES

¾ cup sugar

¾ cup butter or margarine, softened

½ teaspoon vanilla

1 egg

1¾ cups all-purpose flour

3 tablespoons unsweetened baking cocoa

¼ teaspoon salt

ESPRESSO FILLING

¼ cup heavy whipping cream

2 teaspoons instant espresso coffee (dry)

½ bag (11.5-oz size) milk chocolate chips (1 cup)

1 tablespoon coffee-flavored liqueur, if desired

Candy sprinkles or crushed hard peppermint candies, if desired

1 Heat oven to 350°F. In large bowl, beat sugar, butter, vanilla and egg with electric mixer on medium speed, or mix with spoon. Stir in flour, cocoa and salt.

2 Shape dough by rounded teaspoonfuls into 1-inch balls. On ungreased cookie sheet, place balls about 2 inches apart. Press thumb or end of wooden spoon into center of each cookie to make indentation, but do not press all the way to the cookie sheet.

3 Bake 7 to 11 minutes or until edges are firm. Quickly remake indentations with end of wooden spoon if necessary. Immediately remove from cookie sheet to cooling rack. Cool completely, about 30 minutes.

4 Meanwhile, in 1-quart saucepan, heat whipping cream and coffee over medium heat, stirring occasionally, until steaming and coffee is dissolved. Remove from heat; stir in chocolate chips until melted. Stir in liqueur. Cool about 10 minutes or until thickened. Spoon rounded ½ teaspoon filling into indentation in each cookie. Top with candy sprinkles.

1 Cookie: Calories 90 (Calories from Fat 45); Total Fat 5g (Saturated Fat 2.5g); Cholesterol 15mg; Sodium 40mg; Total Carbohydrate 10g (Dietary Fiber 0g); Protein 1g

See photo on page 61.

Holiday Melting Moments

About 3½ dozen cookies

Prep Time: **1 Hour 15 Minutes**   Start to Finish: **2 Hours 45 Minutes**

COOKIES

1 cup butter, softened (do not use margarine)

1 egg yolk

1 cup plus 2 tablespoons all-purpose flour

½ cup cornstarch

½ cup powdered sugar

2 tablespoons unsweetened baking cocoa

⅛ teaspoon salt

VANILLA FROSTING

1 cup powdered sugar

2 tablespoons butter or margarine, softened

1 teaspoon vanilla

2 to 3 teaspoons milk

2 candy canes, about 6 inches long, finely crushed

1 In large bowl, beat 1 cup butter and egg yolk with electric mixer on medium speed, or mix with spoon. Stir in flour, cornstarch, ½ cup powdered sugar, the cocoa and salt. Cover; refrigerate about 1 hour or until firm.

2 Heat oven to 375°F. Shape dough into 1-inch balls. On ungreased cookie sheet, place balls about 2 inches apart.

3 Bake 10 to 12 minutes or until set but not brown. Remove from cookie sheet to cooling rack. Cool completely, about 30 minutes.

4 In small bowl, mix all frosting ingredients except candy canes with spoon until smooth and spreadable. Frost cookies; sprinkle with crushed candy canes.

1 Cookie: Calories 80 (Calories from Fat 45); Total Fat 5g (Saturated Fat 2.5g); Cholesterol 20mg; Sodium 40mg; Total Carbohydrate 9g (Dietary Fiber 0g; Protein 0g

Sparkling Lemon Snowflakes

6 dozen cookies

Prep Time: **50 Minutes**   Start to Finish: **1 Hour 40 Minutes**

COOKIES

¾ cup butter, softened

¾ cup granulated sugar

2 teaspoons grated lemon peel

1 egg

2¼ cups all-purpose flour

¼ teaspoon salt

GLAZE

2 cups powdered sugar

2 tablespoons lemon juice

2 tablespoons water

¼ cup coarse white sparkling sugar

1 In large bowl, beat butter and granulated sugar with electric mixer on medium speed until light and fluffy. Add lemon peel and egg; beat until well blended. On low speed, gradually beat in flour and salt until well blended.

2 Heat oven to 350°F. On floured surface, roll dough ⅛ inch thick. Cut with lightly floured 2½- to 3-inch snowflake-shaped cookie cutter. On ungreased cookie sheets, place 2 inches apart.

3 Bake 8 to 10 minutes or until cookies just begin to brown. Remove from cookie sheets to cooling racks. Cool completely, about 10 minutes.

4 In small bowl, mix powdered sugar, lemon juice and water. Using small metal spatula, spread glaze on tops of cookies; sprinkle with sparkling sugar. When glaze is dry, store in airtight container.

1 Cookie: Calories 60 (Calories from Fat 20); Total Fat 2g (Saturated Fat 1g); Cholesterol 10mg; Sodium 25mg; Total Carbohydrate 9g (Dietary Fiber 0g); Protein 0g

If you don't have a snowflake-shaped cookie cutter, you can use either a star-shaped or scalloped-edge cutter, and cut small triangles and pieces out of the center to form snowflakes.

Decorate-Before-You-Bake Cookies   6 dozen cookies

Prep Time: **50 Minutes**   Start to Finish: **1 Hour 40 Minutes**

COOKIES	DECORATING MIXTURE
¾ cup butter or margarine, softened	½ cup butter or margarine, softened
½ cup sugar	3 teaspoons milk
1 egg	½ cup all-purpose flour
1¾ cups all-purpose flour	4 drops red food color
½ teaspoon baking soda	4 drops green food color
¼ teaspoon cream of tartar	
¼ teaspoon salt	
2 tablespoons sugar	

1 In large bowl, beat ¾ cup butter and ½ cup sugar with electric mixer on medium speed until light and fluffy. Add egg; beat well. Stir in 1¾ cups flour, the baking soda, cream of tartar and salt. Knead dough into smooth ball. Wrap in plastic wrap; refrigerate until firm, about 1 hour.

2 Meanwhile, in small bowl, mix ½ cup butter, the milk and ½ cup flour with fork until well mixed. Divide mixture in half. Stir red food color into 1 half and green food color into other half. Spoon each mixture into decorating bag fitted with small writing tip; set aside.

3 Heat oven to 375°F. Shape 1 half of the cookie dough into ¾-inch balls. Place balls 2 inches apart on ungreased cookie sheets. In small bowl, measure 2 tablespoons sugar. Dip bottom of glass into sugar, and use to flatten each ball into 1½-inch round. Pipe colored mixture from decorating bags on each cookie in various holiday designs. Repeat with remaining half of dough.

4 Bake 7 to 9 minutes or until set. Immediately remove from cookie sheet to cooling rack.

1 Cookie: Calories 50 (Calories from Fat 30); Total Fat 3.5g (Saturated Fat 2g); Cholesterol 10mg; Sodium 40mg; Total Carbohydrate 5g (Dietary Fiber 0g); Protein 0g

Gingerbread Cookies
About 2½ dozen cookies

Prep Time: **1 Hour 5 Minutes**   Start to Finish: **3 Hours 35 Minutes**

COOKIES

1 cup packed brown sugar
⅓ cup shortening
1½ cups full-flavor molasses
⅔ cup cold water
7 cups all-purpose flour
2 teaspoons baking soda
2 teaspoons ground ginger
1 teaspoon ground allspice
1 teaspoon ground cinnamon

1 teaspoon ground cloves
½ teaspoon salt

DECORATOR'S FROSTING, IF DESIRED

2 cups powdered sugar
2 tablespoons milk or half-and-half
½ teaspoon vanilla
Food color, if desired

1 In large bowl, beat brown sugar, shortening, molasses and water with electric mixer on medium speed, or mix with spoon. Stir in remaining cookie ingredients. Cover; refrigerate at least 2 hours until firm.

2 Heat oven to 350°F. Lightly grease cookie sheet with shortening or cooking spray. Roll one-fourth of dough at a time ¼ inch thick on floured surface. Cut into desired shapes. Place about 2 inches apart on cookie sheet.

3 Bake 10 to 12 minutes or until no indentation remains when touched. Immediately remove from cookie sheet to cooling rack. Cool completely, about 30 minutes.

4 In small bowl, mix all frosting ingredients with spoon until smooth and spreadable. Decorate cookies with frosting and, if desired, colored sugars and candies.

1 (2½-inch) Cookie: Calories 200 (Calories from Fat 25); Total Fat 2.5g (Saturated Fat 0.5g); Cholesterol 0mg; Sodium 135mg; Total Carbohydrate 42g (Dietary Fiber 0g); Protein 3g

When using cookie cutters that have one wide end and one narrow end, alternate the placement of it as you cut out the cookies. In other words, cut the first cookie with the wide end of the cutter toward you, then cut the next cookie with the narrow end toward you. This way, you can get more cookies out of one batch of dough.

Top to bottom:
Gingerbread Cookies
and Espresso Thumbprint
Cookies (page 56)

Chocolate Spritz Reindeer

5 dozen cookies

Prep Time: **1 Hour**   Start to Finish: **1 Hour 15 Minutes**

1 cup butter, softened	1 egg yolk
½ cup powdered sugar	2 cups all-purpose flour
½ cup packed brown sugar	60 large pretzel twists
¼ cup unsweetened baking cocoa	60 miniature candy-coated chocolate baking bits
3 tablespoons milk	120 miniature chocolate chips
1 teaspoon vanilla	

1 Heat oven to 375°F. In large bowl, beat butter with electric mixer on medium speed until light and fluffy. Beat in sugars and cocoa until well blended. Beat in milk, vanilla and egg yolk. On low speed, slowly beat in flour until well blended, scraping bowl occasionally.

2 Fit heart template in cookie press; fill cookie press with dough. Place pretzels on lightly floured surface. Force dough through template on top of flat, bottom end of each pretzel twist (two rounds at top of pretzel will form the antlers). Press 2 baking bits at upper part of heart to make eyes, and 1 chocolate chip to make nose on each reindeer. Place reindeer on ungreased cookie sheet.

3 Bake 8 to 10 minutes or until cookies are firm, but not browned. Remove from cookie sheet to cooling rack. Cool completely, about 15 minutes.

1 Cookie: Calories 130 (Calories from Fat 40); Total Fat 4.5g (Saturated Fat 2.5g); Cholesterol 10mg; Sodium 240mg; Total Carbohydrate 21g (Dietary Fiber 1g); Protein 2g

If you don't have a cookie press, shape dough into 1¼-inch balls. Press 1 ball over bottom of 1 pretzel, pinching bottom in to form nose.

These cookies get their name from the word "spritzen," which is German for "to squirt or spray."

Chocolate-Raspberry Triangles

{ 48 triangles }

Prep Time: **30 Minutes**   Start to Finish: **1 Hour 50 Minutes**

1½ cups all-purpose flour

¾ cup sugar

¾ cup butter or margarine, softened

1 package (10 oz) frozen raspberries in syrup, thawed, drained

¼ cup orange juice

1 tablespoon cornstarch

¾ cup miniature semisweet chocolate chips

1 Heat oven to 350°F. In small bowl, mix flour, sugar and butter until crumbly. Press in ungreased 13 × 9-inch pan. Bake 15 minutes.

2 Meanwhile, in 1-quart saucepan, mix raspberries, orange juice and cornstarch. Heat to boiling, stirring constantly. Boil and stir 1 minute. Cool 10 minutes.

3 Sprinkle chocolate chips over crust. Carefully spread raspberry mixture over chocolate chips.

4 Bake about 20 minutes or until raspberry mixture is set. Refrigerate about 1 hour or until chocolate is firm. For triangles, cut into 4 rows by 3 rows, then cut each square into 4 triangles.

1 Triangle: Calories 70 (Calories from Fat 35); Total Fat 3.5g (Saturated Fat 2.5g); Cholesterol 10mg; Sodium 20mg; Total Carbohydrate 10g (Dietary Fiber 0g); Protein 0g

Peppermint Shortbread Bites

64 cookies

Prep Time: **25 Minutes**   Start to Finish: **2 Hours**

1 cup butter, softened (do not use margarine)	3 tablespoons finely crushed hard peppermint candies (about 6 candies)
½ cup powdered sugar	1 tablespoon granulated sugar
2 cups all-purpose flour	3 oz vanilla-flavored candy coating (almond bark), melted
1 teaspoon peppermint extract	

1 In large bowl, beat butter and powdered sugar with electric mixer on medium speed until fluffy. On low speed, beat in flour and peppermint extract.

2 On ungreased cookie sheet, pat dough into 6-inch square, about ¾ inch thick. Cover; refrigerate 30 minutes.

3 Heat oven to 325°F. On cookie sheet, cut dough into 8 rows by 8 rows, making 64 squares. With knife, separate rows by ¼ inch.

4 Bake 28 to 35 minutes or until set and edges are just starting to turn golden. Meanwhile, in small bowl, mix crushed candy and granulated sugar. In small resealable food-storage plastic bag, place melted candy coating. Seal bag; cut tiny hole in corner of bag.

5 Do not remove cookies from cookie sheet. Pipe candy coating over cookies. Before candy coating sets, sprinkle candy mixture over cookies. Remove from cookie sheet to cooling racks. Cool completely, about 30 minutes.

1 Cookie: Calories 50 (Calories from Fat 30); Total Fat 3.5g (Saturated Fat 2g); Cholesterol 10mg; Sodium 20mg; Total Carbohydrate 5g (Dietary Fiber 0g); Protein 0g

To crush candy, place in a resealable freezer plastic bag and seal, then pound with the flat side of a meat mallet or a rolling pin.

These cookies will keep their shape better during baking if they're very cold when you put them in the oven.

Chocolate-Peppermint Shortbread { 32 cookies }

Prep Time: **15 Minutes**   Start to Finish: **1 Hour 10 Minutes**

SHORTBREAD

1 cup butter or margarine, softened

½ cup granulated sugar

4 oz bittersweet baking chocolate, melted, cooled

½ teaspoon peppermint extract

2¼ cups all-purpose flour

⅓ cup unsweetened baking cocoa

GLAZE AND TOPPING

½ cup powdered sugar

2 tablespoons unsweetened baking cocoa

1 to 2 tablespoons milk

2 tablespoons chopped miniature peppermint candy canes

1   Heat oven to 325°F. Spray 2 (9-inch) glass pie plates with cooking spray.

2   In large bowl, beat butter, granulated sugar, chocolate and peppermint extract with electric mixer on medium speed until light and fluffy. On low speed, beat in flour and ⅓ cup cocoa. Divide dough in half. With lightly floured hands, press dough evenly in pie plates.

3   Bake 22 to 24 minutes or until edges just begin to pull away from sides of pie plates. Cool in pie plates on cooling rack 5 minutes. Carefully cut each round into 16 wedges. Cool completely in pie plates on cooling rack, about 30 minutes.

4   In small bowl, mix powdered sugar, 2 tablespoons cocoa and enough of the milk until glaze is smooth and thin enough to drizzle. Drizzle glaze over wedges; sprinkle with candies.

1 Cookie: Calories 140 (Calories from Fat 70); Total Fat 8g (Saturated Fat 5g); Cholesterol 15mg; Sodium 45mg; Total Carbohydrate 15g (Dietary Fiber 1g); Protein 1g

Chocolate-Peppermint Creams

75 pieces

Prep Time: **45 Minutes**   Start to Finish: **1 Hour**

1 bag (12 oz) semisweet chocolate chips (2 cups)

1 bag (12 oz) dark chocolate chips (2 cups)

⅓ cup whipping cream

1 cup butter

¼ cup dry pudding mix from 1 box (4-serving size) vanilla pudding and pie filling mix (not instant)

½ cup whipping cream

½ teaspoon peppermint extract

½ teaspoon vanilla

1 bag (2 lb) powdered sugar

½ cup coarsely chopped peppermint candy canes

1 Spray 15 × 10 × 1-inch pan with cooking spray. Reserve ½ cup of the semisweet chocolate chips. In 2-quart saucepan, heat remaining semisweet chocolate chips, the dark chocolate chips and ⅓ cup whipping cream over medium-low heat, stirring constantly, until melted. Pour into pan; spread evenly. Refrigerate.

2 Meanwhile, in 3-quart saucepan, heat butter, pudding mix and ½ cup whipping cream to boiling over medium heat, stirring constantly. Remove from heat; stir in peppermint extract, vanilla and powdered sugar, beating well, until mixture is smooth. Spread evenly over cooled chocolate layer; freeze until firm, about 15 to 20 minutes.

3 Place reserved ½ cup chocolate chips in small resealable freezer plastic bag. Microwave on High 45 to 55 seconds, turning bag over after 30 seconds. Squeeze bag until chips are melted and smooth. Cut small tip off one corner of bag, and drizzle over top. Immediately sprinkle with chopped candy. Cut into 15 rows by 5 rows.

1 Piece: Calories 140 (Calories from Fat 50); Total Fat 6g (Saturated Fat 3.5g); Cholesterol 10mg; Sodium 25mg; Total Carbohydrate 21g (Dietary Fiber 0g); Protein 0g

decadent desserts

Candy Cane Cake { 16 servings }

Prep Time: **15 Minutes**   Start to Finish: **2 Hours 10 Minutes**

CAKE

1 box (1 lb 2.25 oz) white cake mix with pudding in the mix

1¼ cups water

⅓ cup vegetable oil

3 egg whites

½ teaspoon red liquid food color

½ teaspoon peppermint extract

VANILLA GLAZE

1 cup powdered sugar

1 to 2 tablespoons milk

½ teaspoon regular vanilla or clear vanilla

1 Heat oven to 350°F. Generously grease 10- to 12-cup fluted tube cake pan with shortening (do not spray with cooking spray); lightly coat with flour. Make cake mix as directed on box, using water, oil and egg whites. Pour about 2 cups batter into pan. Into small bowl, pour about ¾ cup batter; stir in food color and peppermint extract. Carefully pour pink batter over white batter in pan. Carefully pour remaining white batter over pink batter.

2 Bake 38 to 42 minutes or until toothpick inserted in center comes out clean. Cool 10 minutes in pan on cooling rack. Remove from pan to wire rack or heatproof serving plate. Cool completely, about 1 hour.

3 In small bowl, mix powdered sugar, 1 tablespoon milk and the vanilla. Stir in additional milk, 1 teaspoon at a time, until smooth and consistency of thick syrup. Spread glaze over cake, allowing some to drizzle down side. Store loosely covered at room temperature.

1 Serving: Calories 210 (Calories from Fat 70); Total Fat 7g (Saturated Fat 2g); Cholesterol 0mg; Sodium 230mg; Total Carbohydrate 33g (Dietary Fiber 0g); Protein 2g

> Start with a cake mix and some red food color, and you end up with a white-and-red-swirled cake that's perfect for your next potluck. This cake transports very well, and don't forget to pack a knife and spatula for serving.

Snowman Cake

12 to 16 servings

Prep Time: **30 Minutes**   Start to Finish: **2 Hours 15 Minutes**

1 box (1 lb 2.25 oz) white cake mix with pudding in the mix

1¼ cups water

⅓ cup vegetable oil

3 egg whites

2 candy canes, unwrapped

2 flat-bottom ice-cream cones

Vanilla-flavored candy coating (almond bark), melted

1 container (1 lb) vanilla creamy ready-to-spread frosting

1 bag (7 oz) flaked coconut (about 2⅔ cups)

5 large black gumdrops

1 large orange gumdrop

7 small black gumdrops

2 pretzel rods

1   Heat oven to 350°F. Grease bottoms only of 2 (8- or 9-inch) round pans with shortening or cooking spray. Make cake mix as directed on box, using water, oil and egg whites. Pour into pans.

2   Bake 8-inch rounds 27 to 32 minutes, 9-inch rounds 23 to 28 minutes, or until toothpick inserted in center comes out clean. Cool 10 minutes; remove from pans to cooling rack. Cool completely, about 1 hour.

3   Cover large flat tray or piece of cardboard with foil. Attach candy cane to open end of each cone, using melted candy coating, to make ice skates; let stand until set. Arrange cake rounds with sides touching on tray. Frost top and sides of cake with frosting. Sprinkle with coconut, pressing gently so it stays on frosting.

4   Use large black gumdrops for eyes and buttons, large orange gumdrop for nose and small black gumdrops for mouth. Arrange pretzel rods for arms and cones for feet with ice skates. Store loosely covered at room temperature.

1 Serving: Calories 540 (Calories from Fat 220); Total Fat 25g (Saturated Fat 11g); Cholesterol 0mg; Sodium 480mg; Total Carbohydrate 76g (Dietary Fiber 1g); Protein 3g

Outfit your snowman with earmuffs and a scarf. For earmuffs, place a creme-filled chocolate sandwich cookie on each side of the snowman's head, and connect them across the top of the head with black string licorice. For the scarf, any flavor of chewy fruit snack (from 3-foot roll) will work.

Bûche de Noël | 10 servings |

Prep Time: **40 Minutes**   Start to Finish: **1 Hour 25 Minutes**

CAKE

3 eggs

1 cup granulated sugar

⅓ cup water

1 teaspoon vanilla

¾ cup all-purpose flour

1 teaspoon baking powder

¼ teaspoon salt

FILLING

1 cup heavy whipping cream

2 tablespoons granulated sugar

1½ teaspoons instant coffee granules or crystals

CHOCOLATE BUTTERCREAM FROSTING

⅓ cup unsweetened baking cocoa

⅓ cup butter or margarine, softened

2 cups powdered sugar

1½ teaspoons vanilla

1 to 2 tablespoons hot water

GARNISH

½ cup chopped green pistachio nuts

1   Heat oven to 375°F. Line 15 × 10 × 1-inch pan with foil or waxed paper; grease with shortening or cooking spray. In small bowl, beat eggs with electric mixer on high speed about 5 minutes or until very thick and lemon colored. Pour eggs into large bowl; gradually beat in 1 cup granulated sugar. Beat in ⅓ cup water and the vanilla on low speed. Gradually add flour, baking powder and salt, beating just until batter is smooth. Pour into pan, spreading batter to corners.

2   Bake 12 to 15 minutes or until toothpick inserted in center comes out clean. Immediately loosen cake from edges of pan; invert onto towel generously sprinkled with powdered sugar. Carefully remove foil. Trim off stiff edges of cake if necessary. While hot, carefully roll cake and towel from narrow end. Cool on cooling rack at least 30 minutes.

3 In chilled medium bowl, beat all filling ingredients on high speed until stiff. Unroll cake; remove towel. Spread filling over cake. Roll up cake.

4 In medium bowl, beat cocoa and butter on low speed until thoroughly mixed. Beat in powdered sugar until mixed. Beat in vanilla and enough of the hot water until frosting is smooth and spreadable.

5 For tree stump, cut off a 2-inch diagonal slice from one end of cake. Attach stump to one long side using 1 tablespoon frosting. Frost cake with remaining frosting. With tines of fork, make strokes in frosting to look like tree bark. Garnish with nuts.

1 Serving: Calories 420 (Calories from Fat 170); Total Fat 18g (Saturated Fat 10g); Cholesterol 105mg; Sodium 180mg; Total Carbohydrate 58g (Dietary Fiber 2g); Protein 5g

Get rave reviews with this beautiful holiday cake! The translation of this recipe title is "Yule log." It's a traditional French Christmas cake shaped and decorated to look like a log. The typical finishing touches include mushroom-shaped baked meringues and "moss" made of chopped pistachio nuts. The time-consuming task of making the mushroom decoration isn't included here, but go ahead and decorate your masterpiece any way you please.

Red Velvet Cupcakes with Marshmallow Buttercream Frosting { 24 servings }

Prep Time: **40 Minutes**   Start to Finish: **1 Hour 30 Minutes**

CUPCAKES

2¼ cups all-purpose flour

¼ cup unsweetened baking cocoa

1 teaspoon salt

½ cup butter or margarine, softened

1½ cups granulated sugar

2 eggs

1 bottle (1 oz) red food color (about 2 tablespoons)

1½ teaspoons vanilla

1 cup buttermilk

1 teaspoon baking soda

1 tablespoon white vinegar

MARSHMALLOW BUTTERCREAM FROSTING

1 jar (7 oz) marshmallow creme

1 cup butter or margarine, softened

2 cups powdered sugar

1 Heat oven to 350°F. Line 24 regular-size muffin cups with paper baking cups. In small bowl, mix flour, cocoa and salt; set aside. In large bowl, beat ½ cup butter and granulated sugar with electric mixer on medium speed until mixed. Add eggs; beat 1 to 2 minutes or until light and fluffy. Stir in food color and vanilla.

2 Beat in flour mixture alternately with buttermilk on low speed just until blended. Beat in baking soda and vinegar until well blended. Divide batter evenly among muffin cups (about ⅔ full).

3 Bake 20 to 22 minutes or until toothpick inserted in center of cupcake comes out clean. Remove from pan to cooling racks. Cool completely, about 30 minutes.

4 Remove lid and foil seal from jar of marshmallow creme. Microwave on High 15 to 20 seconds to soften. In large bowl, beat marshmallow creme and 1 cup butter with electric mixer on medium speed until smooth. Beat in powdered sugar until smooth. Spoon 1 heaping tablespoon frosting onto each cupcake, swirling frosting with back of spoon.

1 Serving: Calories 280 (Calories from Fat 110); Total Fat 12g (Saturated Fat 6g); Cholesterol 50mg; Sodium 250mg; Total Carbohydrate 39g (Dietary Fiber 0g); Protein 2g

Add a little holiday cheer to each cupcake with a holly sprig. Make two holly leaves by splitting one green spearmint leaf candy in half horizontally, and add 3 red cinnamon candies for berries. Or top frosted cupcakes with a snowy drift of flaked coconut.

Hot Chocolate Cupcakes   12 cupcakes

Prep Time: **20 Minutes**   Start to Finish: **1 Hour 25 Minutes**

1¾ cups devil's food cake
  mix with pudding in the mix
  (from 1 lb 2.25-oz box)

½ cup water

3 tablespoons vegetable oil

1 egg

1 cup vanilla creamy ready-to-
  spread frosting (from 12-oz
  container)

½ cup marshmallow creme

¼ teaspoon unsweetened
  baking cocoa

6 miniature pretzel twists,
  broken in half

1 Heat oven to 350°F (325°F for dark or nonstick pan). Place paper baking cup in each of 12 regular-size muffin cups.

2 In large bowl, beat cake mix, water, oil and egg with electric mixer on low speed 30 seconds. Beat on medium speed 2 minutes, scraping bowl occasionally. Divide batter evenly among muffin cups.

3 Bake 17 to 22 minutes or until toothpick inserted in center comes out clean. Cool in pan 10 minutes; remove from pan to cooling rack. Cool completely, about 30 minutes.

4 In small bowl, mix frosting and marshmallow creme. Spoon into small resealable food-storage plastic bag; seal bag. Cut ⅜-inch tip off corner of bag. (Or spoon mixture onto cupcakes instead of piping.)

5 Pipe 3 small dollops of frosting mixture on top of each cupcake to resemble melted marshmallows. Sprinkle with cocoa. Press pretzel half into side of each cupcake for cup handle.

1 Cupcake: Calories 240 (Calories from Fat 80); Total Fat 9g (Saturated Fat 2.5g); Cholesterol 20mg; Sodium 300mg; Total Carbohydrate 37g (Dietary Fiber 0g); Protein 2g

If you like peppermint, frost these fun cupcakes with the frosting mixture, and sprinkle the tops with crushed candy canes.

Cherry-Almond Torte

12 servings

Prep Time: **20 Minutes**   Start to Finish: **3 Hours 10 Minutes**

1 box (1 lb) white angel food
  cake mix

1¼ cups cold water

½ teaspoon almond extract

1 cup marshmallow creme

1 can (21 oz) cherry pie filling

¼ cup sliced almonds,
  toasted*

1 Move oven rack to lowest position (remove other racks). Heat oven to 350°F. Make cake mix as directed on box, using cold water and adding almond extract with the water. Pour into ungreased 10-inch angel food (tube) cake pan.

2 Bake 37 to 47 minutes or until top is dark golden brown and cracks feel very dry and not sticky. Do not underbake. Immediately turn pan upside down onto glass bottle until cake is completely cool, about 2 hours.

3 Run knife around edges of cake; remove from pan. Cut cake to make 2 layers. (To cut, mark side of cake with toothpicks and cut with long serrated knife.)

4 On serving plate, place bottom layer. Spoon ⅔ cup of the marshmallow creme by heaping teaspoonfuls onto bottom layer. Spoon 1 cup of the pie filling between spoonfuls of marshmallow creme. Sprinkle with half of the almonds. Place other layer on top. Spoon remaining marshmallow creme and pie filling on top of cake, allowing pie filling to drizzle down sides. Sprinkle with remaining almonds. Store covered in refrigerator.

*To toast almonds, heat oven to 350°F. Spread nuts in ungreased shallow pan. Bake 6 to 10 minutes, stirring occasionally, until light brown. Or cook nuts in ungreased heavy skillet over medium heat 5 to 7 minutes, stirring frequently until nuts begin to brown, then stirring constantly until light brown.

1 Serving: Calories 240 (Calories from Fat 15); Total Fat 1.5g (Saturated Fat 0g); Cholesterol 0mg; Sodium 280mg; Total Carbohydrate 51g (Dietary Fiber 1g); Protein 4g

Fudgy Brownie Trifle | 20 servings

Prep Time: **15 Minutes**   Start to Finish: **6 Hours 15 Minutes**

1 box (1 lb 2.3 oz) fudge
brownie mix

¼ cup water

⅔ cup vegetable oil

2 eggs

1 tablespoon instant coffee
granules or crystals

1 box (4-serving size)
chocolate fudge instant
pudding and pie filling mix

2 cups cold milk

1 bag (10 oz) toffee bits

1 container (8 oz) frozen
whipped topping, thawed

Chocolate-dipped
strawberries, if desired

Mint sprigs, if desired

1 Heat oven to 350°F. Grease bottom only of 13 × 9-inch pan with shortening or cooking spray. In medium bowl, stir brownie mix, water, oil and eggs until well blended. Stir coffee granules into batter. Spread in pan.

2 Bake 28 to 30 minutes or until toothpick inserted 2 inches from side of pan comes out almost clean. Cool completely, about 1 hour 30 minutes.

3 Cut brownies into 1-inch squares. In bottom of 3-quart glass bowl, place half of the brownie squares. Make pudding mix as directed on package for pudding, using milk. Pour half of the pudding over brownies in bowl. Top with half each of the toffee bits and whipped topping. Repeat with remaining brownies, pudding, toffee bits and whipped topping.

4 Cover and refrigerate at least 4 hours before serving. Store covered in refrigerator. Garnish with fresh mint sprigs.

1 Serving: Calories 320 (Calories from Fat 150); Total Fat 16g (Saturated Fat 6g); Cholesterol 35mg; Sodium 250mg; Total Carbohydrate 39g (Dietary Fiber 1g); Protein 3g

See how easy it is to make the trifle by viewing the video at www.bettycrocker.com/trifle.

Pumpkin Pie   8 servings

Prep Time: **30 Minutes**   Start to Finish: **3 Hours 45 Minutes**

PASTRY

1 cup all-purpose flour

½ teaspoon salt

⅓ cup plus 1 tablespoon
   shortening

2 to 3 tablespoons cold water

PIE

2 eggs

½ cup sugar

1 teaspoon ground cinnamon

½ teaspoon salt

½ teaspoon ground ginger

⅛ teaspoon ground cloves

1 can (15 oz) pumpkin (not
   pumpkin pie mix)

Whipped cream, if desired

1   In medium bowl, mix flour and ½ teaspoon salt. Cut in
shortening, using pastry blender or crisscrossing two knives,
until particles are size of small peas. Sprinkle with cold
water, 1 tablespoon at a time, tossing with fork until all flour
is moistened and pastry almost leaves side of bowl (1 to 2
teaspoons more water can be added if necessary).

2   Gather pastry into a ball. Shape into flattened round on lightly
floured surface. Wrap flattened round of pastry in plastic
wrap and refrigerate about 45 minutes or until dough is firm
and cold, yet pliable. This allows the shortening to become
slightly firm, which helps make the baked pastry more flaky.
If refrigerated longer, let pastry soften slightly before rolling.

3   Heat oven to 425°F. Roll pastry on lightly floured surface, using
floured rolling pin, into round 2 inches larger than 9-inch glass
pie plate. Fold pastry into fourths; place in pie plate. Unfold and
ease into dish, pressing firmly against bottom and side. Flute
edge of pastry in pie plate as desired.

4 Carefully line pastry with a double thickness of foil, gently pressing foil to bottom and side of pastry. Let foil extend over edge to prevent excessive browning. Bake 10 minutes; carefully remove foil and bake 2 to 4 minutes longer or until pastry just begins to brown and has become set. If crust bubbles, gently push bubbles down with back of spoon.

5 Meanwhile, in medium bowl, beat eggs slightly with whisk or hand beater. Beat in remaining pie ingredients except whipped cream.

6 Cover edge of pie crust with 2- to 3-inch strip of foil to prevent excessive browning; remove foil during last 15 minutes of baking. To prevent spilling filling, place pie plate on oven rack. Pour pumpkin mixture into hot pie crust.

7 Bake 15 minutes. Reduce oven temperature to 350°F. Bake about 45 minutes longer or until knife inserted in center comes out clean. Cool on wire rack 2 hours. Serve with whipped cream. After cooling, pie can remain at room temperature up to an additional 4 hours, then should be covered and refrigerated.

1 Serving: Calories 240 (Calories from Fat 110); Total Fat 12g (Saturated Fat 3g); Cholesterol 55mg; Sodium 310mg; Total Carbohydrate 29g (Dietary Fiber 2g); Protein 4g

Be sure to use canned pumpkin, not pumpkin pie mix, in this recipe. The mix has sugar and spices already in it, so if you have purchased the pumpkin pie mix, follow the directions on that label.

See photo on page 89.

Pecan Pie   8 servings

Prep Time: **30 Minutes**   Start to Finish: **1 Hour 20 Minutes**

Pastry (page 86)	3 eggs
⅔ cup sugar	1 cup pecan halves or broken pecans
⅓ cup butter or margarine, melted	Whipped cream, if desired
1 cup corn syrup	Chopped pecans, if desired
½ teaspoon salt	

1 Heat oven to 375°F. Make Pastry, using 9-inch glass pie plate and following steps 1, 2 and 3 of Pumpkin Pie recipe.

2 In medium bowl, beat sugar, butter, corn syrup, salt and eggs with whisk or hand beater until well blended. Stir in pecan halves. Pour into pastry-lined pie plate.

3 Bake 40 to 50 minutes or until center is set. Serve pie with whipped cream and chopped pecans.

1 Serving: Calories 530 (Calories from Fat 260); Total Fat 29g (Saturated Fat 8g); Cholesterol 100mg; Sodium 420mg; Total Carbohydrate 62g (Dietary Fiber 2g); Protein 5g

Chocolate-Pecan Pie Melt 2 oz unsweetened baking chocolate with the butter.

Cranberry-Pecan Pie Stir in 1 cup dried cranberries with the pecan halves.

Peanut–Chocolate Chip Pie Substitute 1 cup salted peanuts for the pecans. After baking, sprinkle with ½ cup semisweet chocolate chips.

For a pie crust with a twist, braid the edge. Loosely braid three ¼-inch pastry strips (from trimmed pastry), making the braid long enough to fit along the edge of the pie. Moisten edge of pie and place braid on top, pressing lightly to seal.

See how easy it is to make and freeze whipped cream by viewing the how-to video at www.bettycrocker.com/whippedcream.

Left to right: Pecan Pie and Pumpkin Pie (page 86)

Easy Peppermint Dessert { 15 servings }

Prep Time: **55 Minutes**   Start to Finish: **13 Hours 55 Minutes**

1 package (1 lb) creme-filled chocolate sandwich cookies, crushed (about 3 cups)

½ cup butter or margarine, melted

½ gallon peppermint stick, party mint or mint chip ice cream, softened

1 container (12 oz) frozen whipped topping, thawed

½ cup butter or margarine

4 oz unsweetened baking chocolate, chopped

2 cups sugar

1 can (12 oz) evaporated milk

1 teaspoon vanilla

⅓ cup crushed peppermint candies or candy canes

1 In medium bowl, mix crushed cookies and ½ cup melted butter. Press mixture firmly in bottom of ungreased 13 × 9-inch pan.

2 In large bowl, stir together ice cream and 2 cups of the whipped topping; spoon evenly over cookie crust. Freeze about 3 hours or until firm.

3 Meanwhile, in 2-quart saucepan, melt ½ cup butter and the chocolate over low heat, stirring constantly. Stir in sugar; gradually stir in milk. Heat to boiling over medium-high heat, stirring constantly. Cook and stir 5 minutes or until slightly thickened; stir in vanilla. Cool completely, about 2 hours.

4 Pour 2 cups of the chocolate sauce evenly over ice cream. Freeze at least 8 hours but no longer than 2 weeks. Cover and refrigerate remaining sauce.

5 Reheat reserved sauce until just warm. To serve, cut into 5 rows by 3 rows. Top with sauce and remaining whipped topping; sprinkle with crushed candies.

1 Serving: Calories 680 (Calories from Fat 340); Total Fat 37g (Saturated Fat 20g); Cholesterol 75mg; Sodium 380mg; Total Carbohydrate 79g (Dietary Fiber 4g); Protein 8g

{ To soften the ice cream, place it in the refrigerator for 30 minutes. }

Lindy's Cheesecake

16 to 20 servings

Prep Time: **45 Minutes**   Start to Finish: **15 Hours**

CRUST

1 cup all-purpose flour

½ cup butter or margarine, softened

¼ cup sugar

1 egg yolk

CHEESECAKE

5 packages (8 oz each) cream cheese, softened

1¾ cups sugar

3 tablespoons all-purpose flour

1 tablespoon grated orange peel, if desired

1 tablespoon grated lemon peel, if desired

¼ teaspoon salt

5 eggs

2 egg yolks

¼ heavy whipping cream

GARNISH

¾ heavy whipping cream

⅓ cup slivered almonds, toasted (page 82)

1 Heat oven to 400°F. Lightly grease 9-inch springform pan with shortening; remove bottom. In medium bowl, mix all crust ingredients with fork until dough forms; gather into a ball. Press one-third of the dough evenly in bottom of pan. Place on cookie sheet. Bake 8 to 10 minutes or until light golden brown; cool. Assemble bottom and side of pan; secure side. Press remaining dough 2 inches up side of pan.

2 Heat oven to 475°F. In large bowl, beat cream cheese, 1¾ cups sugar, 3 tablespoons flour, the orange peel, lemon peel and salt with electric mixer on medium speed about 1 minute or until smooth. Beat in eggs, 2 egg yolks and ¼ cup whipping cream on low speed until well blended. Pour into crust.

3 Bake 15 minutes. Reduce oven temperature to 200°F. Bake 1 hour longer. Cheesecake may not appear to be done; if a small area in the center seems soft, it will become firm as cheesecake cools. (Do not insert a knife to test for doneness because the hole could cause cheesecake to crack.) Turn off oven; leave cheesecake in oven 30 minutes longer. Remove from oven and cool in pan on wire rack away from drafts 30 minutes.

4 Without releasing or removing side of pan, run metal spatula carefully along side of cheesecake to loosen. Refrigerate uncovered about 3 hours or until chilled; cover and continue refrigerating at least 9 hours but no longer than 48 hours.

5 Run metal spatula along side of cheesecake to loosen again. Remove side of pan; leave cheesecake on pan bottom to serve. In chilled small bowl, beat ¾ cup whipping cream with electric mixer on high speed until stiff. Spread whipped cream over top of cheesecake. Decorate with almonds and lemon peel. Store covered in refrigerator.

1 Serving: Calories 520 (Calories from Fat 350); Total Fat 39g (Saturated Fat 23g); Cholesterol 220mg; Sodium 310mg; Total Carbohydrate 35g (Dietary Fiber 0g); Protein 9g

Chocolate Chip Lindy's Cheesecake Fold 1 cup miniature semisweet chocolate chips (3 oz) into cheese mixture before pouring into crust. Drizzle each serving with caramel and chocolate ice cream topping, and sprinkle with toasted pecan halves, if desired.

CLICK!

See how easy it is to freeze cheesecake slices by viewing the video at www.bettycrocker.com/freezecheesecake.

metric conversion guide

volume

U.S. Units	Canadian Metric	Australian Metric
¼ teaspoon	1 mL	1 ml
½ teaspoon	2 mL	2 ml
1 teaspoon	5 mL	5 ml
1 tablespoon	15 mL	20 ml
¼ cup	50 mL	60 ml
⅓ cup	75 mL	80 ml
½ cup	125 mL	125 ml
⅔ cup	150 mL	170 ml
¾ cup	175 mL	190 ml
1 cup	250 mL	250 ml
1 quart	1 liter	1 liter
1½ quarts	1.5 liters	1.5 liters
2 quarts	2 liters	2 liters
2½ quarts	2.5 liters	2.5 liters
3 quarts	3 liters	3 liters
4 quarts	4 liters	4 liters

weight

U.S. Units	Canadian Metric	Australian Metric
1 ounce	30 grams	30 grams
2 ounces	55 grams	60 grams
3 ounces	85 grams	90 grams
4 ounces (¼ pound)	115 grams	125 grams
8 ounces (½ pound)	225 grams	225 grams
16 ounces (1 pound)	455 grams	500 grams
1 pound	455 grams	0.5 kilogram

NOTE: The recipes in this cookbook have not been developed or tested using metric measures. When converting recipes to metric, some variations in quality may be noted.

measurements

Inches	Centimeters
1	2.5
2	5.0
3	7.5
4	10.0
5	12.5
6	15.0
7	17.5
8	20.5
9	23.0
10	25.5
11	28.0
12	30.5
13	33.0

temperatures

Fahrenheit	Celsius
32°	0°
212°	100°
250°	120°
275°	140°
300°	150°
325°	160°
350°	180°
375°	190°
400°	200°
425°	220°
450°	230°
475°	240°
500°	260°

Recipe Index